Miles of Style

Eunice W. Johnson and the EBONY Fashion Fair

by Lisa D. Brathwaite

illustrations by Lynn Gaines

Lee & Low Books Inc.
New York

Dedicated to Besty, Beverly, and Bella—three generations of
women who have influenced my style. For little Kellie Minor,
and all the sparkly ones like her.
—L. D. B.

To my mom, Anna, my creative fashion inspiration!
—L. G.

Eunice made her first grand entrance in 1916, as the second child born to the Walker family of Selma, Alabama. Her mother was an art teacher and school administrator. Her daddy was a doctor, caring for Black people in their tight-knit community.

The family's home was an elegant display of personal style. Oil paintings hung in the parlor. Fancy plates were used to set the dinner table. Even the broad oak and chinaberry trees that lined their road were stately.

Beauty was Eunice's birthright, and she grew up believing that beauty and dignity were things everyone should experience.

Young Eunice loved to sew.
She designed clothes for her dolls
because she liked them to be well
dressed. Her friends agreed that
Eunice had a flair for fashion.
As the girls played, the dolls could
be anyone and go anywhere Eunice
imagined. There were no rules in her
fashion world.

Soon Eunice was crafting clothes for herself and designing shirts for
Daddy too. They had collars that stood up and buttonholes sewn by hand.
He was proud to wear the shirts when he served his patients.

In high school, Eunice entered local sewing contests. Determined to produce prize-winning pieces, she ripped out uneven seams and did them over and over again until they were straight as arrows. Eunice impressed the judges with her attention to detail, and she won many of the competitions.

When Eunice earned her high school diploma, she also received certificates in sewing and tailoring. She wondered how she could use her talents and style to serve others.

Mother and Daddy supported Eunice's interest in sewing and fashion, but they also valued hard work and learning. "If you want to make a difference in this world, you must first get an education," Daddy always said. So, Eunice enrolled at Alabama's Talladega College. She soon graduated with a degree in sociology and headed to Loyola University in Chicago, where she studied for an additional degree in social work.

One night at a dance, Eunice met John H. Johnson, a young businessman. Sparks flew between them as they shared their ideas about Black life and success.

Eunice returned to Selma to marry John in 1941. Her wedding dress was detailed to perfection. It gathered and flowed like spring water, spilling into a rippling pool at her feet.

Back in Chicago, Eunice and John were happy. But they noticed newspapers and magazines often printed stories that showed Black people in a negative light. The newlyweds came up with a groundbreaking idea. They would publish a magazine that featured positive news about Black Americans and their communities.

John tried to get a bank loan to advertise the magazine. Many bankers said no because he was Black. He was finally able to borrow five hundred dollars by offering his mother's furniture as a promise to pay back the loan.

The Johnson Publishing Company was born. Eunice worked as a social worker during the day and for the company at night. The new magazine, *Negro Digest*, published its first issue in November 1942. It quickly became a success.

Three years later, John and Eunice launched their company's second publication, *EBONY*. Eunice named the monthly magazine for ebony, the strong, fine wood prized for its deep and gleaming black color. With a bold title and fetching cover photographs, *EBONY* showed images of Black Americans that were more alluring and inspiring than what readers were used to seeing on newsstands. Inside, the magazine was filled with articles and more pictures that celebrated Black life, culture, and achievements.

People couldn't wait to snatch up a copy!

Eunice believed readers would also be interested in fashion articles, so she began writing a style column called "Fashion Fair." In the column, Eunice shared her love of fashion and design, and she showcased new clothing trends on stunning Black models. Sometimes Eunice shuttled the models to fascinating faraway places for photographs that would be featured in the magazine. She was certain when readers saw models who looked like them in exciting settings, they would imagine themselves enjoying similar adventures.

One day in 1958, Jessie Covington Dent, a friend from New Orleans, asked Eunice and John for a favor. Mrs. Dent wanted to raise money for a local hospital. She knew a group of women who would pay to attend a fashion show with models like the ones in *EBONY*. Would Eunice and John help her organize the show?

Eunice liked the idea. She could be of service by showcasing style for Black women who had been ignored by the fashion establishment. She would bring the beauty to them in an up-close, personal, and profitable way. Here was her chance to make a difference in the world the way she'd always wanted.

Eunice and the *EBONY* staff got to work preparing the show. They planned every detail, selecting the models and choosing the clothes and accessories.

On the day of the show, the venue buzzed with excitement. Decked out in the latest styles, the models strutted back and forth on the stage with poise and precision. Their power and pride pulsed through the audience as the models merrily swiveled in colors society had said they couldn't wear against their brown skin. Rocking reds! Popping purples! Yes, yes, yellows! A new world of style welcomed those who attended the show. They delighted in the experience.

Mrs. Dent and the hospital were delighted too with the money the show raised.

Word spread about the fashion show, and soon other Black organizations asked to host their own events. Eunice and John chose nine more cities for a national tour. Soon the EBONY Fashion Fair traveling show became a major way to raise funds for favorite charities.

Every year, Eunice chose a different concept for the show circuit. The theme she selected for 1963 was "Americana." She wanted the tour to highlight the creations of a select group of American designers as well as famous European ones.

When a key *EBONY* staff member fell ill, Eunice stepped in to produce as well as direct the show. She gathered a team of wardrobe assistants and a show crew. Then she got to work selecting and buying the clothes.

Eunice studied the work of Black designers from across the United States. She tasked the best of them with making magnificent outfits for her models to wear. It was a mission the designers gladly accepted.

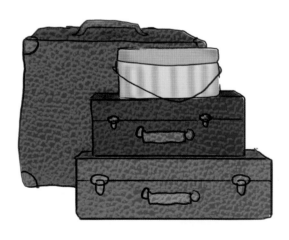

Eunice flew to Paris to attend the fashion shows where top designers displayed their newest collections. Sometimes she was not welcomed. Her brown skin made many uneasy. Some feared white women seeing their fashions on Black models.

The rejection hurt, but Eunice refused to turn and go home. She shared copies of *EBONY* and explained how she would introduce the designers' creations to a new buying market. Surprised but convinced by her determination— and her drive to push past them if necessary—one by one, the fashion houses opened their doors.

Eunice selected pieces she called "showstoppers"—sensational, jaw-dropping outfits to thrill the audiences at home. She looked for quality, fun, and fantasy in each piece. While other fashion-show producers borrowed and returned high-fashion clothes, Eunice paid for them so they were hers to keep!

The EBONY Fashion Fair "Americana" tour took off in September 1963. The first stop was the Diamond Beach Club in Wildwood, New Jersey. The models— nine women and one man who had been selected from a cross-country search—dressed in their outfits for the first of eight scenes that would lead to a grand finale.

Backs straight, heads held high, the graceful models sashayed and posed on the runway to a lively piano accompaniment. Feathers flipped and fluttered. Beachwear blazed and beckoned. Shifting sequins shimmered. The sparkle from jewels jumped in the light. A commentator's witty quips added to the excitement.

What a show!

From Wildwood, the Fashion Fair zigzagged across the country to sixty-six more cities. The models, Fashion Fair staff, and the clothes all traveled together in a renovated Greyhound bus. While the show was glamorous, life on the road was sometimes difficult. The reception they received was not always warm and welcoming. In the South, they encountered restrooms, hotels, and restaurants that would not allow them in because they were Black. Eunice often called on local families to provide places for the models and staff to spend the night. Sometimes the white bus driver went into restaurants to order meals, and then everyone ate on the bus.

Despite the hardships, Eunice saw to it that the Fashion Fair continued on its course. The show was the event of the year for Black style-seekers. Crowds gathered to catch glimpses of the models coming off the bus. City leaders welcomed them. Young girls pranced and posed like the proud models. From high school gymnasiums to theaters to grand ballrooms, audiences dressed in their Sunday best to watch all the glamour on the runway.

The EBONY Fashion Fair "Americana" show reached its last stop in Los Angeles, December 1963. By then it had traveled more than thirteen thousand miles. The tour had been cheered by audiences and praised by newspapers as a triumphant testament to fashion, culture, creativity, and consciousness.

Eunice went on to design even larger and grander EBONY Fashion Fair extravaganzas. More cities were added. More dates were added. More causes were supported. More body types were celebrated. With each season she discovered many talented young women and men and helped them launch careers in fashion and other industries. By the time the tours ended in 2009, the shows had raised tens of millions of dollars for Black charities and scholarships.

Eunice Walker Johnson used her elegance, power, and influence to inspire her community by showcasing the strength and beauty she knew lived within it. As she reflected that beauty with delight and dignity, the world couldn't help but notice her style!

1975

1987

1996

2007

Author's Note

Eunice Walker Johnson was someone whom today we would call an "influencer"—a person who used her prominence in the media to influence popular tastes and culture. In her day she was best known for directing the EBONY Fashion Fair and for her featured column in *EBONY* magazine. But "Mrs. Johnson," as she was reverently referred to by all, was an extraordinary lifestyle expert across many fields. Fashion, beauty, travel, art—Mrs. Johnson introduced the Black community and wider American society to these topics through a melanated lens, extending an invitation to come along for the VIP experience.

She was best known for her influence in fashion, where she had an eye for picking superstars early in their careers. Through the EBONY Fashion Fair, she elevated the profiles of Black designers like Stephen Burrows, B Michael, Patrick Kelly, and Willi Smith. She supported and befriended young designers long before they built iconic brands like Valentino, Cavalli, Pierre Cardin, and Yves Saint Laurent. In the end, more than four thousand EBONY Fashion Fair shows in the United States and the Caribbean lifted audiences to a higher fashion consciousness.

EBONY Fashion Fair in Chicago, IL, 1978.

Mrs. Johnson brought her same eye for talent and beauty to interior design and to visual art. She minored in art in college and studied interior design in Chicago. She later put those skills on full display in outfitting the Johnson Publishing Company headquarters at 820 S. Michigan Avenue. The headquarters featured many pieces from Mrs. Johnson's broad art collection. Legendary EBONY Fashion Fair commentator Audrey Smaltz recalled being introduced to artist Pablo Picasso by Mrs. Johnson on one of their many European buying trips. The building that houses the headquarters was designated a Chicago landmark in 2017.

EBONY Fashion Fair in Chicago, IL, 1978.

When something that was necessary for beauty didn't exist, Mrs. Johnson created it. She was appalled when she discovered her EBONY Fashion Fair models had to mix foundation shades not suited for their skin tones to make up their faces for the runway. She went to cosmetics companies to make a case for a solution. When they didn't move fast enough, she and Mr. Johnson gathered their own team of experts and launched Fashion Fair Cosmetics, providing yet another way for Black models—and the people they inspired—to authentically look their best. At its peak, it was the largest Black cosmetics line in the world.

Mrs. Johnson championed beauty as well as brilliance.
She believed that success in life began with a good education and
this philosophy was a central pillar in her work. Under her tutelage
EBONY Fashion Fair models, staff, and crew members went on
to build successful careers and leave their own mark in fashion
and other related sectors like film, television, print media, and
production.

During its five-decade long
run, the EBONY Fashion Fair raised
more than fifty-five million dollars
making scholarships possible
for countless students. Mrs.
Johnson received many awards
acknowledging her innumerable
contributions to institutes of
higher learning—including a
Lifetime Achievement Award from
UNCF (the United Negro College
Fund) and honorary degrees from
Shaw University and her alma
mater Talladega College.

EBONY Fashion Fair in Chicago, IL, 1978.

Eunice W. Johnson (left) standing next to a model
at the Ebony Fashion Fair in Chicago, IL, 1977.

In 2013, the Chicago
History Museum debuted
*Inspiring Beauty: 50 Years of
Ebony Fashion Fair*, a special
exhibition built around a
curation of Mrs. Johnson's
vast couture clothing
collection that showcased
the history and substance
of the traveling tour.
The showing was eagerly
anticipated and attended by
throngs of participants, many
of whom shared recollections
of their show experiences.
As with the EBONY Fashion
Fair, demand for the exhibition grew, resulting in its traveling to
additional museums across the United States.

**Mrs. Johnson was an exemplary fashion and philanthropic
pioneer.** The Metropolitan Museum of Art in New York City
planned a tribute luncheon in her honor to be held in January 2010.
Regrettably, Mrs. Johnson died on January 3, 2010. However, the
luncheon was still held just over a week later. Her daughter, Linda
Johnson Rice, and granddaughter, Alexa Christina Rice, joined A-list
dignitaries, fashion luminaries, and other celebrities in reflecting on
Mrs. Johnson's fifty-plus years of contributions to American culture
and society.

After some financially turbulent years, *EBONY* magazine was
purchased in 2020 by former NBA basketball player Ulysses "Junior"
Bridgeman. A successful businessman, Bridgeman expressed the
feelings of many when his new ownership was announced: "When
you look at *EBONY*, you look at the history not just for Black people,
but of the United States. I think it's something that a generation is
missing and we want to bring that back as much as we can."

I carry fond childhood memories of thumbing through the
magazine's issues that graced my family's coffee table. I'd mimic
the models, holding my head high. I'm hopeful *EBONY*'s cultural
legacy built by John H. Johnson and Eunice W. Johnson will
continue to flourish and inspire future generations.

PHOTO CREDITS

p. 36 (left): 1978: ST-90002904-0022, Chicago Sun-Times collection, Chicago History Museum

p. 36 (right): 1978: ST-90002904-0023, Chicago Sun-Times collection, Chicago History Museum

p. 37 (left): 1978: ST-90002904-0111, Chicago Sun-Times collection, Chicago History Museum

p. 37 (right): 1977: ST-90002884-0038, Chicago Sun-Times collection, Chicago History Museum

QUOTATION SOURCE

p. 10: "If you . . . an education." Nathaniel D. Walker, quoted in "UNCF Honors Ebony Fashion Fair Producer/Director: JPC Secretary-Treasurer Eunice W. Johnson receives organization's highest Award," *Ebony*, June 2001: 96. https://books.google.com/books?id=ENoDAAAAMBAJ&q=Nathaniel+Walker#v=onepage&q=Nathaniel%20Walker&f=false

AUTHOR'S SOURCES
BOOKS AND ARTICLES

"Backstage." Editorial, *Ebony*, June 1963: 23. https://books.google.com/books?id=riksVFZN9XsC&pg=PA23&dq=Fashion+Fair+Americana&hl=en&sa=X&ved=0ahUKEwiQxYmIkufNAhWDVyYKHbskAm0Q6AEIMzAD#v=onepage&q=Fashion%20Fair%20Americana&f=false

"Backstage." Editorial, *Ebony*, October 1963: 23. https://books.google.com/books?id=X_WsIHH8ugEC&pg=PA23&dq=Fashion+Fair+Americana&hl=en&sa=X&ved=0ahUKEwiQxYmIkufNAhWDVyYKHbskAm0Q6AEIKzAB#v=onepage&q=Fashion%20Fair%20Americana&f=false

"Backstage." Editorial, *Ebony*, February 1988: 28. https://books.google.com/books?id=ocwDAAAAMBAJ&lpg=PA28&dq=Nathaniel+Walker&pg=PA28#v=onepage&q=NathanielWalker&f=false

Bailey, Eric J. 2008. *Black America, Body Beautiful: How the African American Image Is Changing Fashion, Fitness, and Other Industries*. Westport, CT: Praeger.

Buchanan, Gwendolyn, ed. "Ebony Fashion Show." Editorial, *Tiger's Roar*: Savannah State College [Savannah] November 1963, 18, no. 2 (sec. 5). Internet Archive. LYRASIS Members and Sloan Foundation. http://www.archive.org/details/tigersroar196365sava

Chaplin, Julia. "A Runway Fair That Still Packs the House." *The New York Times*, October 14, 2001. http://www.nytimes.com/2001/10/14/style/a-runway-fair-that-still-packs-the-house.html

Chicago History Museum, Joy L. Bivins, and Rosemary K. Adams. 2013. *Inspiring Beauty: 50 Years of Ebony Fashion Fair*. Chicago: Chicago Historical Society.

Cleveland, Pat, and Lorraine Glennon. 2016. *Walking with the Muses: A Memoir*. New York: Atria, Simon & Schuster.

"Decades of Fashion: Ebony Fashion Fair—Then and Now." *Jet*, December 17, 2001: 34–39. https://books.google.com/books?id=3rUDAAAAMBAJ&pg=PA34&dq=Ebony,+Ebony+Fashion+Fair,+Eunice+Johnson,+1964&hl=en&sa=X&ved=0ahUKEwjijebb7rnNAhUG4CYKHan7Bh4Q6AEIHjAA#v=onepage&q&f=false

"Ebony Fashion Fair Celebrates 33rd Anniversary." *Ebony*, April 1991: 110+. https://books.google.com/books?id=0MsDAAAAMBAJ&lpg=PA114&dq=Eunice+Walker,+dolls&pg=PA114#v=onepage&q=EuniceWalker,dolls&f=false

"Ebony's New Fashion Fair Commentator: 'Ginny' Tibbs Helps Guide 67-City Tour." *Jet*, September 26, 1963: 41. https://books.google.com/books?id=d8EDAAAAMBAJ&lpg=PA41&dq=Elaine%20Johnson&pg=PA41#v=onepage&q=Elaine%20Johnson&f=false

"Eunice W. Johnson: A Life Well Lived 1916–2010." *Ebony*, March 2010: 86–108.

"Fall and Winter Styles in Fashion Fair." *Ebony*, November 1963: 155+. https://books.google.com/books?id=zvkMMATVAnwC&pg=PA155&dq=Fashion+Fair+Americana&hl=en&sa=X&ved=0ahUKEwiQxYmIkufNAhWDVyYKHbskAm0Q6AEINzAE#v=onepage&q=Fashion%20Fair%20Americana&f=false

"Fashion Fair Americana." *Ebony*, September 1963: 195+. https://books.google.com/books?id=WF2MuN467ZIC&pg=PA195&dq=Fashion+Fair+Americana&hl=en&sa=X&ved=0ahUKEwiQxYmIkufNAhWDVyYKHbskAm0Q6AEIJzAA#v=onepage&q=Fashion%20Fair%20Americana&f=false

Horyn, Cathy. "Eunice Johnson and the Best Dressed List." *The New York Times*, August 3, 2012. https://archive.nytimes.com/runway.blogs.nytimes.com/2012/08/03/eunice-johnson-and-the-best-dressed-list

Jefferson, Margo. 2016. *Negroland: A Memoir*. New York: Vintage.

Johnson, John H., and Lerone Bennett. 1989. *Succeeding Against the Odds*. New York: Warner.

"Medic Who Delivered 5,000 Selma Babies Dies in Chicago." *Jet*, June 3, 1971: 22. https://books.google.com/books?id=ojcDAAAAMBAJ&lpg=PA22&dq=Dr.%20Nathaniel%20Walker&pg=PA22#v=onepage&q=Dr.%20Nathaniel%20Walker&f=false

Muhammad, Claudette Marie. 2006. *Memories*. Chicago: FCI.

Norment, Lynn. "Defining Fabulous: Celebrating 50 Years of the Ebony Fashion Fair." *Ebony*, September 2007: 110–15. https://books.google.com/books?id=rdMDAAAAMBAJ&pg=RA1-PA13&dq=Fashion+Fair+Americana&hl=en&sa=X&ved=0ahUKEwiQxYmIkufNAhWDVyYKHbskAm0Q6AEILzAC#v=onepage&q=Fashion%20Fair%20Americana&f=false

Swanstrom, Mary Anne. "An Evening of Style." *The Huntsville Times*, AL.ABAMA Media Group, January 6, 2008. http://blog.al.com/enjoy/2008/01/an_evening_of_style.html

"UNCF Honors Ebony Fashion Fair Producer/Director." *Ebony*, June 2001: 94–96. https://books.google.com/books?id=ENoDAAAAMBAJ&lpg=PA96&dq=Nathaniel+Walker&pg=PA94#v=onepage&q=NathanielWalker&f=false

PHOTOGRAPHS AND VIDEOS

Eunice W. Johnson Tribute Luncheon. Dir. Christopher Noey. Prod. Christopher Noey. With Former President Bill Clinton; Desirée Rogers, White House Social Secretary; Thomas P. Campbell, Director of The Metropolitan Museum of Art; Emily K. Rafferty, Met President; Linda Johnson Rice, Ebony Chairman and CEO; Harold Koda, Curator in Charge of The Costume Institute; Donna Williams, Met Chief Audience Development Officer. Metropolitan Museum of Art. Made Possible in Part by Macy's, June 23, 2011. https://www.youtube.com/watch?v=09ysze0SoTo

The Vision of Eunice Johnson. Prod. Zero One Projects, Joy L. Bivens, Daniel Oliver, Alex Aubry, Tamara Biggs, and John Russick. Dir. Nat Soti. Perf. Linda Johnson Rice, Kenneth Marlon Owen, Audrey Smaltz, Pat Cleveland, B M. Chicago History Museum, 2013. YouTube. TCW Magazine, May 1, 2013. https://www.youtube.com/watch?v=AcoSwVGuJoY

Unknown. Multiple photos. 1963. Freedom House Photographs: Roxbury People, Places, and Events, 1950–1975, Northeastern University Libraries, Box 65, Folder 2713, Boston.

SHOW PROGRAMS AND AUCTION CATALOGS

The 1963 Ebony Fashion Fair Americana. Chicago: Johnson, 1963. Show program provided to the author courtesy of Edward C. Hirschland, President, The Landhart Corporation.

Leslie Hindman Auctioneers. "Property from the Ebony Fashion Fair Collection." Issuu, January 1, 1965. https://issuu.com/lesliehindman/docs/153_ebony

Leslie Hindman Auctioneers. "Sale 236: Property from the Ebony Fashion Fair Collection." Issuu, January 1, 1966. https://issuu.com/lesliehindman/docs/236

INTERVIEWS

Carrington, Gwen C. Selma native and neighbor of Eunice W. Johnson's Walker family. Telephone interview with the author, June 15, 2016.

Dawson, Verdell Lett, Ed.D. Selma native and friend of Eunice W. Johnson's Walker family. Telephone interview with the author, July 1, 2016.

Morrow, Mary. Reference librarian, Selma Dallas County Public Library. Email correspondence with the author, June–July 2016.

Muhammad, Claudette Marie. 1963 Ebony Fashion Fair model. Telephone interview with the author, July 12, 2016.

Parrish, Athelstein Sullivan. Childhood friend of Eunice W. Johnson. Telephone interview, July 15, 2016.

Wright, A. J., MLS. Retired medical librarian, University of Alabama at Birmingham. Email correspondence with the author, January 2019; June 2016.

ACKNOWLEDGMENTS

Writing a children's book is no small feat. Tremendous thanks to . . .

Kandace Coston, for shepherding this book to completion, and to editors Cheryl Klein and Louise May for their roles as well.

Lynn Gaines for contributing her artistic gift and making my inner child's heart swoon.

Those connected–directly or indirectly–to Mrs. Johnson who helped me navigate her past, so I could share about her in my present, and leave it for generations of the future: Gwen C. Carrington; Edward C. Hirschland; Verdell Lett Dawson, Ed.D.; Claudette Marie Muhammad; Athelstein Sullivan Parrish, by way of Alfrae Johnson and Alan Sidransky; Audrey Smaltz.

The gifted researchers, archivists, and librarians who lent their expertise and support: Lisa Moore; Mary Morrow; A.J. Wright; We Need Diverse Books for noting my work and connecting me with Patricia Hruby Powell, a mentor first and a friend for life; my Decatur Chill Writers Group friends, who read or listened to my drafts and gave fitting feedback.

Team Brathwaite, present for the New Voices Award congratulatory call and joining me on the subsequent roller coaster ride, holding my hand and enduring my varying cries; Isabella's LPA friends, who can now buy the book she told them her mommy was writing. The dear others–friends and family–who may not appear here by name, but whose support I've cherished.
Thank you, everyone.

Library of Congress Cataloging-in-Publication Data
Names: Brathwaite, Lisa D., author. | Gaines, Lynn, illustrator.
Title: Miles of style : Eunice W. Johnson and the Ebony Fashion Fair / by Lisa D. Brathwaite ; illustrated by Lynn Gaines.
Description: First edition. | New York : Lee & Low Books Inc., [2024] | Includes bibliographical references. | Audience: Ages 6–11 | Summary: "The life work of Eunice W. Johnson, co-founder of Ebony magazine and a visionary who championed Black elegance through the Ebony Fashion Fair—a cross-country fashion show fundraiser"—Provided by publisher.
Identifiers: LCCN 2023007915 | ISBN 9781620143124 (hardcover) | ISBN 9781620149904 (ebk)
Subjects: LCSH: Johnson, Eunice Walker, 1916–2010—Juvenile literature. | Fashion designers—United States—Biography—Juvenile literature. | African American fashion designers—Biography—Juvenile literature. | Women fashion designers—United States—Biography—Juvenile literature. | Ebony (Chicago, Ill.)—Juvenile literature. | African Americans—Clothing—Juvenile literature. | African Americans—Clothing—Exhibitions—Juvenile literature. | Clothing and dress—United States—History—20th century—Juvenile literature. | Fashion—United States—History—20th century—Juvenile literature.
Classification: LCC HD9940.U4 J6437 2024 | DDC 338.7/687092 [B]—dc23/eng/20230531
LC record available at https://lccn.loc.gov/2023007915